POIN[...]

TO THE

PAST

The origin of Halstead street names

Michael Bardell

Mike Bardell
3.VI.03

First published in 2003

by

Michael Bardell MA
381 Cressing Road
Braintree
Essex
CM7 3PE

ISBN 0 9529105 2 7

Printed by

PressXpress
Fox Meadow
23 Courtauld Road
Braintree
Essex
CM7 9BD

By the same author:

"A Sense of Place, the origin of Braintree & Bocking street names"
"The Military Volunteers of Braintree & Bocking" (Limited production)
"Give Them Ale Enough, a history of Braintree & Bocking pubs"

INTRODUCTION

"Roads go on
While we forget, and are
Forgotten like a star
That shoots and is gone."

Edward Thomas, poet, killed at Arras, 1917

Everyone notices street names because they figure so prominently in our daily lives but as the nature, and even the history, of a town is to some degree encapsulated therein, a modicum of local knowledge is necessary to determine their origin. The reader may pause here to consider why a Braintreeite should produce a book about Halstead – to this I shall return. Halstead street names, like those in any town, are an eclectic mix of old rural and modern urban titles. Many medieval names are now a distortion of their original form while others represent a language, and indeed a life, quite different to our own; Mallows Field and Chipping Hill would be examples in Halstead.

The town's oldest roads would have been tracks through the forest as prehistoric people moved westward from the coast along high ground. People settled on these tracks, particularly where they crossed, and Halstead developed along what are now the Colchester to Cambridge, Braintree to Sudbury routes. As major landholders hemmed in the town with their large estates, so the gardens, backyards, and eventually whole areas between the roads, were built up. Later sheer pressure necessitated the erosion of estate land and gradually farmland disappeared under urban development.

When few people could read or write it was sufficient simply to describe a road. This could be done in various ways, by direction for example North Street (now Hedingham Road), after a prominent building like Box Mill Lane, or by geophysical means like Mount Hill. Eventually the size of a town would render this method inadequate – "Head Street opposite the Rose and Crown" – becoming practically useless as the yards and backland in that area filled up. But the crucial factor was the introduction, in 1840, of the Penny Post and the subsequent phenomenal growth of letter writing. In Braintree, by way of example, we learn that on 2 October 1861 "*Mr Smoothy gave notice that he would at the next meeting bring before the Board* (of Health - a precursor of local government) *the naming of streets and the numbering of the houses.*" Doubtless the same happened in Halstead.

Today naming is largely an arbitrary exercise with few stated policies; tastes too have changed. Honouring of prominent citizens is on the wane but sadly addresses that sound "nice" are in vogue. Thankfully local historians are increasingly asked to make suggestions and although land is swallowed up at an alarming rate, names in touch with the past often remain for posterity.

Halstead has always held an important place in my heart. As a child I enjoyed holidays with my Aunt Bertha at the Radio Relay in Head Street and visits to the "top playing field". My great aunt Nellie was for fifty-five years first nanny then family friend to the Frost's at North Mill. Her mother, my maternal great-grandmother, ended her days in a cottage behind 21 High Street before war broke out in 1939. From 1971 to 1973 I worked for Alan Bragg the architect in Hedingham Road but my most important Halstead connection is my marriage thirty-two years ago in Holy Trinity Church to Linda Mitson, born and bred in Mitchell Avenue; my mother-in-law, to whom this book is dedicated, still lives there.

There is a degree of conjecture in the writing of local history and I am solely responsible for the hypotheses contained in this book. If any reader cares to submit corrections, additional information or other pertinent material this would be gratefully received. While the judgements are mine I have benefited from the advice and help of several people. My mother-in-law Mrs Thelma Mitson, brother Dr Peter Bardell, Ken Stanhope and Stan Haines; Janet Pring and Beryl Ricketts of Braintree District Council and staff at the Essex Record Office, Chelmsford. My particular thanks go to Doreen Potts whose cheerful and prompt responses to innumerable questions were a blessing.

Michael Bardell, Braintree December 2002

GAZETTEER

Abels Road
Abel de St Martin bought the Halstead estate in the reign of Henry II or King John and his family held it until 1312. The manor house stood in the area now occupied by 29 and 31 Hedingham Road.

Acorn Avenue
Tree and woodland names simply seem to be an attempt to conjure up visions of leafy suburbia and occur in many towns! Halstead has many, particularly on the most modern and densely developed estates! However not all fall into this category. (cf Oak Road, Orchard Avenue and The Pippins).

Adams Court
Thomas Adams bought the Stanton Grey Trinity Street brewery in 1876 and some of the buildings remain next to the Braintree District Council office, itself the Adams' home.

Apple Tree Close
See Acorn Avenue.

Ash Rise
See Acorn Avenue.

Ashlong Grove
A property developer called van Ash bought land at the Howe from the Courtauld family; his solicitor was A R Long of Wayman and Long, Clare – hence Ashlong.

Balls Chase
Ball's farmhouse still stands although the datestone of 1867 must indicate a refurbishment since the building is listed late-18th century.

Bays Drive
Baize, a fine woollen cloth, one of the "new draperies" introduced by Flemish refugees after 1560, was woven extensively in north Essex.

Beech Avenue
See Acorn Avenue.

Belle Vue Terrace
Common in many towns, simply a location with an agreeable vista.

Bentall Close
The name of Bentall's Farm in Sudbury Road is a mid-17th century corruption of the 14th century Brendon Hall, later Brenthall.

Beridge Road
Reverend Basil Beridge, rector of Gosfield, owned the land on which this road was built.

Birch Drive
See Acorn Avenue.

Blackthorns
Perhaps the hedgerows in this area contained sloe trees? (Prunus spinosa) Many in Essex do.

Blamsters Crescent
The manor of Blomsters or Blampsters takes its name from John de Blaumuster of 1286.

Bluebridge Industrial Estate
The bridge itself was painted blue by John Morley (cf Morley Road) a notorious practical joker in 1722. An alternative theory is that "blue" is a corruption of "below" – the bridge beyond, or downstream, of the town.

Boisfield Terrace/Bois Hall Gardens
The name Bois derives from John de Bosco or De Bois of 1233. The manor originally subservient to Abels became Halstead's chief manor; the building was replaced circa 1605 by Bois Hall which in turn was demolished in the late 1960's.

Bourchier Way
Boys Hall manor was held by Lord Bourgchier in the reign of Edward III although the name is as old as the Norman Conquest – Bowser then later de Burser or de Bousser.

Bourne Close
Bourne Brook rises near Wethersfield airfield, passes through Gosfield Lake and crosses the Braintree-Halstead road between Pennypots and Russels Road. It was La Burnebroke in 1275, Le Boorneby 1344.

Box Mill Lane
There were three Halstead mills recorded in Domesday Book. One was at Box Mill Lane, later there were two here, a windmill in use until 1882 and a water mill which survived until 1926.

Bridge Street
The chief bridge in the parish – Town Bridge – a ford before the mill was erected which partly stopped the water, rendering wading impractical.

Brook Farm Close
Brook Farm house still stands alongside Colchester Road. (This should not be confused with Brook Street Farm on the westerly edge of the parish nearly into Hedingham.) Due to the building of Blue Bridge Industrial Estate the brook has largely been contained in a culvert. However it emerges at the former railway bridge abutment and then runs down into the River Colne.

Brook Place
Believed to commemorate another small brook that ran down to the Colne from the Abels Road area.

Broton Drive
Broton Properties Ltd developed this industrial estate in the late 1970's.

Butler Road
R A Butler was Saffron Walden Constituency MP for thirty-nine years and one-time Minister for Education and Chancellor of the Exchequer. He lived for many years at Stansted Hall. This street was called Trinity Square until 1968.

Cangle
Le Cangle-Hatch marks the boundary with Pebmarsh. The name probably derives from the Latin "cancelli" meaning enclosure, barrier or railings.

Causeway
When the Colne crossing was a ford this would have been a marshy area; the river banks were probably raised to provide both flood protection and a dry passage. Technically a causeway is paved with limestone hence the medieval latin "via calciata" from which the names derives.

Chapel Hill
First mentioned in 1413, a chapel dedicated to the Honour of the Holy Trinity stood where roads to Braintree and Gosfield meet. Foundations of triangular shape, discovered in William Holman's day (cf Holman road) led people to believe that the chapel was three-sided but it is now assumed these supported a wall surrounding a conventional shaped building.

Chapel Street/Upper Chapel Street
High Street Congregational Church stood on the corner of High Street and Chapel Street and was taken down so the Post Office could be built in 1964, its members having merged with Parsonage Street Congregational in 1946.

Cherry Tree Close
See Acorn Avenue.

Chipping Hill
The Old English for market is "cēping" and until mid-13th century the market took place in this area.

Churchill Avenue
Built around the time Sir Winston Churchill died in 1965. (cf Winston Way)

Clare Close
William the Conqueror bestowed land at Halstead on Richard Fitz-Gilbert, Earl of Brion in Normandy and Lord of Clare in Suffolk.

Clovers
Owen Clover of Earls Colne took over the former House of Correction in Bridge Street 1871 and converted it into a flour mill. It closed in 1965.

Coggeshall Pieces/Coggeshall Way
Land along Colchester Road was owned by a Coggeshall trust, the bequest of Sir Robert Hitcham who died in the 17th century. This was administered by Pembroke College, Cambridge for educational purposes. However the name probably precedes this era, there having been one William de Coggeshale owning Halstead land in 1298. By the reign of Edward VI the Coggeshall family owned "Munchensies" near Blue Bridge (cf Morley Road).

Colchester Road
Self-explanatory.

Colne Road
The River Colne rises just below the bridge near the back entrance to Moyns Park on the Steeple Bumpstead to Stambourne Road. Officially 32 miles long to its tidal limit at Colchester East Mill the name's origin is obscure and is thought simply to mean "water" or "river".

Colne Valley Close
Self-explanatory.

Colne View
Self-explanatory.

Conies Road
Conies Farm still stands along Oak Road. Coney is another name for rabbit and these were once "farmed" as a meat supply. The Halstead farms of The Wash and Donjohns both had fields called "Coney Burrow" in the 1838 Tithe Award.

Conway Close
Built by H C Janes Ltd a Luton developer who always named their estates after places in Britain.

Cooks Close
The Cooks have been a large and multi-branched Halstead family since the Wars of the Roses. Perhaps two of the better known members are William Cook, 1824-1911, a builder, developer, malster and publican, and George Cook who started brewing in Parsonage Street in 1885, a business that removed to Tidings Hill Brewery in 1908.

Courtaulds Close
Little need be said about this family of Huguenot refugees and goldsmiths-cum-silk weavers who founded a huge international textile enterprise. Arriving in Halstead in 1825 Samuel Courtauld & Co was the town's largest employer for generations.

Cutting Drive
Jack Cutting councillor, last Chairman of Halstead Urban District Council until it was subsumed into Braintree District Council in 1974.

De Veres Road
The de Vere family flourished in Essex from the Norman Conquest until the death of the 20th Earl of Oxford in 1703. Hedingham Castle was their home for 600 years. (cf Oxford Road).

Dooley Road
This is a field name derived from "dal" meaning portion or share of land, especially in a common field. By the 13th century the word often appeared as "dole" and by the 16th century "doule" or "doole".

Dorset Close
Dorset evolved as a preference to the name originally suggested – "Joiners Close which doubtless reflected A R Clarke & Son the builders whose yard it occupies. It actually commemorates the 1st Battalion, the Dorsetshire Regiment which was stationed in, and around, Halstead from early November 1943 to February 1944.

East Mill
In 1800 Isaac Sewell built a smock mill which burnt down sixty-two years later.

Elizabeth Way
Built around the time of the Queen's Silver Jubilee in 1977.

Elm Drive
See Acorn Avenue.

Factory Lane East/Factory Lane West
Courtauld's factory filled the space between these two roads.

Fairfield Way
A guess would be that this commemorates the fair which is held in the field next to the fire station nearby.

Fifth Avenue
Unimaginative numbering of roads on Bluebridge Industrial Estate.

Finsbury Place
Takes its name from Finsbury House, Head Street.

First Avenue
See Fifth Avenue.

Firwoods Road
Firwood House, a Victorian building, demolished in 1961. It had a large fir tree either side of the drive. Its former name was Stone's Grange (cf Grange Close).

Fleece Yard
A pub of this name stood in Hedingham Road.

Fourth Avenue
See Fifth Avenue.

Fenn Road/Upper Fenn Road
An ancient name taken by Robert atte Fenn in 1365. The piece of land called Fenn Ground was divided into three closes in 1639. The junction of Fenn Road and the lane to Colne Engaine was known as Snowden Fenn.

Gardeners Road
Takes its name from the Gardeners Arms pub which was demolished to allow the road to be built. The pub name could be that of its first landlord but may be connected with Sir Thomas Gardiner, Lord of Bois Hall manor in the reign of James I.

Garden Terrace
See Gardeners Road. However the name might simply record the fact that houses were built on the garden of another property.

Gatehouse Yard
This was the entry to the old St Andrew's vicarage grounds but may originally have been the entrance to the substantial manor of Stansted Hall. (cf Stanstead Road).

Godwin Close
Stansted Hall had been held by Godwine, a Saxon freeman, in the reign of Edward the Confessor.

Grange Close
See Firwoods Road.

Great Yard
Appearing on comparatively recent Ordnance Survey maps this insignificant yard off Tidings Hill, just north of the Ronald Road turning, is no longer named.

Harold Close
Named by architect Alan Bragg in memory of his father, the builder, Harold Bragg whose works yard lay behind his bungalow in Middlefield.

Harvey Street
Bridges Harvey lived at Blue Bridge House around the turn of the 20th century and a part of his land was purchased for the erection of Halstead Girls Grammar School in 1907.

Haubourdin Court
The modern conurbation of Lille in France contains in its outer suburbs the town of Haubourdin, twinned with Halstead since 1983. Textiles are still produced in the area – unlike Halstead!

Hawthorn Close
See Acorn Avenue.

Head Street
Common name for a street at the uppermost part of town.

Hedingham Road
Self-explanatory. Known as North Street in the 19th century.

Highbury Terrace
Like Head Street, a name given to a position in the uppermost part of town.

Highfields
This private development was known as the Highfields Estate for marketing purposes.

High Street
For once "high" need not be a term to describe elevation but rather "main" – the expected locality of trade and commerce and often the place where a market was held as indeed it was in Halstead until 1898.

Holman Road
William Holman pastor of the church of Protestant Dissenters in Halstead from 1700 to 1730 was also an historian and antiquary. His writings on the history of Essex eventually passed to Philip Morant whose "History of the Antiquities of the County of Essex" is still an invaluable source for local historians.

Holmes Road
Elizabeth Holmes, spinster, left the considerable legacy of £4,000 per annum in 1783, part of the interest of which was to pay for bread and clothing "*for decayed* (destitute) *housekeepers who have not received parish assistance.*"

Honeywood Road
The Honeywood family of Marks Hall near Coggeshall owned the manor of Stansted Hall in the late 19th century.

Howe Chase
The name derives from the Saxon "hou" – hill – recorded as Le Hoo in 1202.

Johnston Close
Enid Johnston councillor for Greenstead Green in the mid-20th century, lived in the village at Greensteadhall Farm.

Juniper Close
Charlie Juniper councillor, Chairman of Halstead Urban District Council in 1956, churchwarden at Holy Trinity.

Kings Road
Opinion is divided on this name. Firstly, a track developed in 1904 to commemorate the comparatively recently crowned Edward VII; secondly a local builder, John King, who lived at 1 Kings Road around turn of the 20th century. But what about Edmund King, gentleman, who in 1624 gave by his will £100 to purchase land, the rent from which was to be employed in buying bread weekly for the town's poor? I am inclined towards the latter since as early as the 1876 Ordnance Survey this is shown as a road in process of development.

Knowles Road
William Knowles was the local Essex County Council highways surveyor in the mid- 20th century. In his youth he represented his county, Somerset, at rugby.

Kestrel Rise
As wildlife habitat disappears under ever-spreading residential development a sense of the countryside is presumably claimed under bland names like this. (cf Acorn Avenue).

Kingfisher Meadow
See Kestrel Rise.

Lindens
A new development not just adding to the "forest" of tree names (cf Acorn Avenue) as it runs alongside a dwelling called "Linden Lea" whose new owners believe that lime trees grew in this area. In fact other properties with "Linden" in their name stand nearby, reinforcing this assertion. Linden is the Old English name for lime tree.

Link Road
Literally links White Horse Avenue and Abels Road. However Blamsters Farm had a "Link Ley" (field) albeit on the south side of Oak Road opposite Conies Farm in the 1838 Tithe Award.

Lock Road
Bert Lock, councillor, served on Halstead Urban District Council for thirty years and was chairman six times, the first in 1943.

Mallows Field
Robert Malet supported William the Conqueror, held the Barony of Eye in Suffolk and was lord of the manor at Stansted Hall. (cf Stanstead Road).

Manfield
Richard Man had Halstead property circa 1274 and Mann's Farm was said to have belonged to Reynold Manne in 1548. Latterly Manfield belonged to Bois Hall Farm.

Maple Close
See Acorn Avenue.

Martins Road
In 1573 William Martin left land and property for the foundation of a free school and for relief of the poor. A barn for storage of crops deposited as rent in connection with this charity stood about on the corner of today's Martins Road and Kings Road until the end of the 19th century.

Matthews Close
Moreton Matthews headmaster of the British School from 1893 and of the Council School from its inauguration in 1910 was a superb illustrator of old Halstead buildings. (cf Moreton Way).

Mayda Close
Takes its name from "Mayda Terrace" which still exists; it is likely the builder used his children's names, perhaps May and Daniel or David?

Meadows Close
Built close to the River Colne's flood meadows.

Middlefield
This street simply follows the course of a diagonal path which ran across the middle of Pamplins Field.

Mill Chase
Chase indicates a once private road leading to a property, in this case North, or Frost's, Mill. Originally a post mill of early-19th century origin it was replaced by a smock mill on a brick base around one hundred years later. In 1878 there was also a steam mill on site and by 1907 the use of wind power had ceased.

Mitchell Avenue
The first houses in this street were built by the Halstead Co-operative Society. J T W Mitchell of humble parentage was a "Rochdale Pioneer" and went on to become President of the English Co-operative Wholesale Society, from 1874 to 1895. He believed religion, temperance and co-operation to be the three great forces for the improvement of mankind but disagreed with the aristocratic E V Neale not least in the matter of temperance which Mitchell took to mean total abstinence. (cf Neale Road).

J T W Mitchell
1828–1895

Monklands Court
Mr Jackson's dental surgery almost certainly stands on land originally belonging to the chapel and it is possible that monks associated with it lived there. (cf Chapel Hill).

Moreton Way
See Matthews Close.

Morley Road
Halstead born butcher, John Morley was a speculator, man of acute judgement, eccentric and benefactor. In the early-18th century he demolished a dwelling called Munchensies and in its place erected Blue Bridge House which still has a free-stone inlaid in the brickwork over the door with the butchers arms embossed on it. To the end of his life he killed a pig in Halstead market once a year to show that he had not forgotten his trade. (cf Bluebridge Industrial Estate and Coggeshall Pieces/Way).

Mount Hill/Mount Rise
A term normally given to steeply rising ground and thus well named.

Mount Pleasant
While the name suggests an elevated and salubrious locality that is agreeable to live in, it is often given ironically to somewhere noticeably unsavoury or unhealthy. Interestingly a fever hospital was built there circa 1873.

Nash Court
Cyril Nash councillor, member of Halstead Urban District Council from 1962 until 1973 and chairman on three occasions.

Nether Court
Takes its name from the large house Nether Priors which itself occupies the site of a manor subordinate to Abels, held by a family called "Pryors" in "ancient times".

New Street
Any street described as "new" would have been aptly, if unoriginally, descriptive at the time of its construction. However its first name was Berkeley Terrace c1855 and before that Prospect Row.

North Mill Place
See Mill Chase.

Neale Road
Edward Vansittart Neale, Christian socialist and barrister was General Secretary and Legal Advisor of the Co-operative Union and drew up the model rules which regulate its societies. His Oxford University-bred moral intellectualising tended progressively to antagonise co-operators like J T W Mitchell (cf Mitchell Avenue).

Edward Vansittart Neale
1810–1892

Oak Road
Do not refer to Acorn Avenue as this is one tree name which stands apart.

The name commemorates "Blamsters Oak" an ancient tree that stood in the general vicinity of the entrance to Blamsters Farm, opposite Oak Road (which was then called Beakeley Lane). It was cut down in disputed circumstances in the 19th century. Reputedly six yards (5.5 metres) in circumference the tree must have been over 200 years old. Presumably Oak Road and cottages were named to remind the Earl of Mornington, who perpetrated the destruction, of his folly!

Orchard Avenue
Built in an area occupied by several small cottages and known as Orchard Yard. No doubt there was an orchard in the locality at one time.

Oxford Road
See de Veres Road.

Park Drive
A comparatively recent development, given its grand title because it adjoins Kings Road playing field.

Parker Way
Ted Parker councillor, member of Halstead Urban District Council for forty-two years and chairman on three occasions.

Parsonage Street/Parsons Court
It is believed the original St Andrew's Parsonage stood near the river – Parsonage House today. The modern Parsonage stands much more conveniently at the other end of the street, just across from the church.

Paynters Terrace
Paynter's pond, doubtless named after a landowner as early as Edward IV's reign, was the source of water that ran down Head Street and High Street in an open ditch. The pond shows clearly on the 1855 Board of Health plan and was filled once Halstead Water Works were built circa 1862.

Peartree Close
See Acorn Avenue.

Poplar Close
See Acorn Avenue.

Portway Court
Charles Portway and his son were ironfounders who patented the famous Tortoise Slow Combustion Stove. Its invention in 1830 had been intended simply as the means of heating their High Street warehouse but it went on to world acclaim.

Pretoria Road
It was common after the Peninsular, Crimean and Boer Wars to name streets in commemoration of famous battles; the Boer capital Pretoria was entered by British troops on 5 June 1900.

Prior Close
Matthew Prior poet and diplomat was a friend of John Morley (cf Morley Road) and frequent visitor to Halstead staying at Blue Bridge House.

Ramsey Road
Dame Mary Ramsey founded Halstead Grammar School in 1594 for forty free scholars. A great benefactress she was the second wife of Sir Thomas Ramsey, Lord Mayor of London, and died in 1601.

Ravens Avenue
Commemorates "Ravens Meadow". This was not an ancient field name rather land that belonged to the Raven family, owners of Colne Valley Ironworks and agricultural engineers, who had premises in Kings Road until 1935.

Rayner Way
Reginald Rayner served as a local government officer for both Halstead Rural and Urban District Councils, retiring in 1961 after forty-four years service.

River Close
Built close to the River Colne.

Ronald Road
Sir Ronald Long, a local solicitor, and one of only four clerks in the life of Halstead Urban District Council serving over forty years. He was knighted following his year as President of the Law Society in 1964.

Rosemary Lane
This name is old but not ancient since Holman, in his writings of the early-18th century, refers to "Pritchards Lane now called Rosemary Lane". It could be the name of a landowner's wife or daughter or maybe the evergreen shrub used for culinary and perfumery purposes was grown there.

Rose Yard
The name is connected with the Rose and Crown pub, now closed, which was on the opposite side of Head Street. Interestingly another small yard below, and adjacent the pub, was called Crown Yard.

Roundacre
The developer's name for marketing purposes was retained as the street name.

Russels Road
Russell's Farm stands on the east side of this lane, roughly half-way between the Braintree and Gosfield Roads. The name was in use as early as 1341 when John Russel held it.

Rye Hills
Built in the locality of Rye Hill Field, Stones Farm.

St Andrews Road
This has probably been the site of Christian worship since Saxon times, and one associated with pagan rites before that.

Saxon Close
These north-German invaders had a well-established community in Halstead by Domesday. This is probably a "nice-sounding", though not inappropriate, developer's name.

School Chase
Holy Trinity Lower School, an auxiliary of Holy Trinity National School, was opened in 1858 for the convenience of pupils living in the Tidings Hill area; it closed in 1910 and the building is now a dwelling. Called Gilbey's chase on the 1876 Ordnance Survey.

Second Avenue
See Fifth Avenue.

Slate
Not named although still shown on recent street maps. Little more than a path, it led from a point nearly opposite the Griffin pub in an "L" shape round to the swimming pool. "Slate" is the name on a map of 1831, by the 1876 Ordnance Survey it is clearly marked "The Slade" but back to "Slate" on the 1896 and 1922 Ordnance Surveys. While there were a couple of Slade Fields in Halstead, neither were in this vicinity. Perhaps the word is a corruption of the Old English "slæd" meaning, appropriately, low flat valley.

Sloe Hill
Sloe or Slowhouse was known as a manor in 1700. It was held in Saxon times by Wulfwine who was dispossessed at the Norman Conquest, the property bestowed by William the Conqueror on Aubrey de Vere, one of his followers.

Slough Farm Road
Presumably Slough Farm and Sloe Manor are in some way connected. They are close and the name is similar. "Slough" derives from the Old

English "slöh" – meaning mire or bog and perhaps appropriate to this low-laying area.

South Close
Simply a turning – running south off Highfields.

Spansey Court
Sparmesey Springe was a part of Slow House estate in 1567; by the 1876 Ordnance Survey this had become Great and Little Spansey Woods belonging to Cut Hedge and White House Farms.

Stanley Road
Stanley Moger, an auctioneer and estate agent, contested his first council election in 1894 and came bottom of the poll. Undeterred he was elected top of the poll in 1898 and served for many years on the Urban District Council, as chairman in 1934. He was responsible for opening up the Beridge and Stanley Road area for development.

Stanstead Road
See Mallows Field. In 1553 Stansted Hall (Stanstead seems to be the modern spelling) was brick built, it had a centre courtyard, chapel, moat, two storey gate-house and was embattled all round with a turret at each corner. The name records its stony or gravely situation and at one time it was a hamlet separate from Halstead with its own constable, court and poor relief arrangements. It lies one and a half miles to the south-west of the town.

Star Stile
Apparently nothing more ancient than a stair, or ladder, stile in the late-19th century.

Sudbury Road
Self-explanatory.

Symonds Court
Stanley Symonds grocer of Bridge Street from the early 1930's to the 1960's was chairman of Halstead Urban District Council in 1952.

Swallow Walk
See Kestrel Rise.

Taverners Field
Like nearby Raven's Meadow, "Taverner" may have been an owner of this land which now gives access to Fairfield Way off Balls Chase.

The Centre
Unimaginative name for an unimaginative attempt at town centre redevelopment – the shopping centre!

The Pippins
This development covers an orchard belonging to the Allen family, scrap merchants. Pippin can mean an apple grown from seed or simply a red and yellow dessert apple

The Tythings/Tidings Hill
Halstead's most familiar street name to outsiders (thanks to Cook's Brewery!) has proved elusive. "Tidings" may well derive from "tything" – the medieval system whereby groups of ten households were responsible to the manorial court for the conduct of each member. Alternatively the road may have led to tithe land – that which supported the local clergyman. As an outsider how about "tidings", or news, of invasion? During the Armada invasion scare of 1588 a series of fire beacons starting at the south coast would warn people of imminent danger. Presumably the glow from a beacon at Braintree would have been visible from the top of the hill and it is suggestive that a Stones Farm field, opposite the eastern end of Oak Road, is called "Toothill Field" from the Old English "töt" – lookout place.

Third Avenue
See Fifth Avenue.

Three Gates Close
Probably refers to a field that had three entrances.

Trinity Mews/Trinity Road/Trinity Street
Holy Trinity Church, whose dedication commemorates the chapel that stood nearby (cf Chapel Hill), was an early example of the Gothic Revival style by the architect Sir George Gilbert Scott. It cost around £5000 and its first spire fell down when nearing completion in 1844.

Tryon Court
Sir Samuel Tryon of Layer Marney, a family of Huguenot origin, was Lord of Halstead manor in 1620 and rebuilt Bois Hall. His son, also Sir Samuel, was High Sheriff of Essex in 1649 and 1650.

Tweed Close
John Tweed gentleman, lived in High Street in 1688 when his wife and infant son died. At his death he left money for a bread charity to be distributed among sixteen aged poor parishioners.

Tylneys Road
The Lord Viscount Castlemain and Earl Tylney of the Kingdom of Ireland owned Bois Hall and Cangle Hatch in the early-17th century.

Upper Trinity Road
See Trinity Mews/Trinity Road/Trinity Street.

Vicarage Meadow
Stands on the old St Andrew's Vicarage grounds behind the current vicarage. (cf Gatehouse Yard).

Vicarage Court
Built on the site of Holy Trinity Vicarage demolished after the church closed in 1987.

Warren Road
William de Warrena supported William the Conqueror and was rewarded by having land in Halstead bestowed on him.

Weavers Court/Weavers Row
Weavers court is a modern development where Courtauld's factory once stood; Weavers Row is a terrace of mid-19th century three storey mansard roofed weavers cottages that contained large well lit rooms at first floor level for the looms.

Well Fields
Built in the locality of Well Field, Stones Farm.

West Road
Possibly a simple geographic location – a westerly turning off Mitchell Avenue.

West Yard
Similarly this un-named yard today is a westerly turning off Tidings Hill. However it is part of the Cook's Brewery complex and may relate to an important employee.

White Horse Avenue
Blamsters Farm had First and Second White Horse Fields in the 1838 Tithe Award; White Horse Cottages stand in Oak Road on the edge of those fields, now built over.

Willow Way
See Acorn Avenue.

Windmill Road
This field belonging to Blamsters had a mill which was destroyed by fire in 1800.

Winston Way
See Churchill Avenue.

BIBLIOGRAPHY

Primary Sources

General Plan of Halstead for the Board of Health, circa 1855 (Essex Record Office D/DU 371/33)

Kelly's Directory Essex, 1894 and 1937

Ordnance Survey Maps:

1st Edition 1876, scale 1:2500
2nd Edition 1896, scale 1:2500
3rd Edition circa 1922, scale 1:2500
Explorer 195, Braintree & Saffron Walden, 1998, scale 1:25000

Tithe Award for Halstead, 1838 (Essex Record Office D/CT 158A)

Published Sources

Addison, William, *Essex Worthies*, Chichester, Phillimore, 1973.
Backstrom, Phillip N. *Christian Socialism and Co-operation in Victorian England,* London, Croom Helm, 1974.
Bamberger, Percy A. L. *Discover Halstead*, Halstead, Halstead and District Local History Society, 1982.
Bamberger, Percy A. L. *Halstead in Old Picture Postcards*, Netherlands, European Library, 1987.
Clarke, Vernon, *Essex River Colne*, Colne Engaine, Vernon Clarke, 1979.
Copsey, Geoffrey R. *Halstead and the Urban District Council 1894-1974*, Halstead, Halstead and District Local History Society, 1987.
Downey, Mary and Potts, Doreen, *Schools and Scholars in Halstead and District*, Halstead, Halstead and District Local History Society, 1986.
Evans, William James, *Old and New Halstead*, Halstead, 1886.
Field, John, *English Field Names*, Newton Abbot, David and Charles, 1972.
Gibbons, T. G. *Holman's Halstead*, Halstead, W.H. Root, 1909.
Halstead and District Local History Society, *A Pictorial History of Halstead*, Halstead, Halstead and District Local History Society, 1979.

Mawer, A. and Stenton, F. M. eds. *Introduction to the Survey of English Place Names*, Cambridge, Cambridge University Press, 1969.
Medlycott, M. *Origins of Halstead*, Chelmsford, Essex County Council, 2002.
Mills, A. D. *A Dictionary of English Place Names*, Oxford, Oxford University Press, 1991.
Muilman, P. *Muilman's History of Essex, Volume II*, Chelmsford, 1770.
Osborne, David, *Halstead and the Colne Valley*, Stroud, Tempus, 1999.
Pilgrim, John E. "The cloth industry in East Anglia". In *The Wool Textile Industry in Great Britain*, ed. Geraint J. Jenkins, pp 252-268. London, Routledge and Kegan Paul, 1972.
Potts, Doreen, *Halstead's Heritage*, Halstead, Halstead and District Local History Society, 1989.
Reaney, P. H. *The Place-Names of Essex*, Cambridge, University Press, 1969.
Room, Adrian, *The Street Names of England*, Stamford, Paul Watkins, 1992.
Smith, Ken, *Essex Under Arms*, the early years to 1900, Romford, Ian Henry, 1998.
Stokes, H. G. *English Place Names*, London, Batsford, 1948.
Webb, Catherine, ed. *Industrial Co-operation, the Story of a Peaceful Revolution*, Manchester, Co-operative Union, 1912.